Best Easy

Best Easy Day Hikes
Tucson

Second Edition

Bruce Grubbs

FALCON GUIDES

GUILFORD, CONNECTICUT

FALCONGUIDES®

An imprint of Rowman & Littlefield
Falcon and FalconGuides are registered trademarks and Make Adventure Your Story is a trademark of Rowman & Littlefield.

Distributed by NATIONAL BOOK NETWORK

Copyright © 2017 Rowman & Littlefield
TOPO! Maps copyright 2017 National Geographic Partners, LLC.
All Rights Reserved.
Maps © Rowman & Littlefield

British Library Cataloguing-in-Publication Information Available

A previous edition was catalogued as follows by the Library of Congress:

Library of Congress Cataloging-in-Publication Data

Grubbs, Bruce (Bruce O.)
  Best easy day hikes, Tucson / Bruce Grubbs.
     p. cm. — (Falconguides)
  ISBN 978-0-7627-5250-8
  1. Hiking—Arizona—Tucson Region—Guidebooks. 2. Tucson Region (Ariz.)—Guidebooks. I. Title.
  GV199.42.A72T835 2009
  917.91'776—dc22

                                        2009029486

ISBN 978-1-4930-2776-7 (paperback)
ISBN 978-1-4930-2777-4 (e-book)

∞™ The paper used in this publication meets the minimum requirements of American National Standard for Information Sciences—Permanence of Paper for Printed Library Materials, ANSI/NISO Z39.48-1992.

Printed in the United States of America

Contents

Acknowledgments vii
Introduction viii
　Hazards.. ix
　Environmental Considerations xiii
How to Use This Book xv
Trail Finder xix
Map Legend xx

THE HIKES

Tucson Mountains
　1. Picacho Peak 3
　2. Picture Rocks Wash..................................... 6
　3. Signal Hill Trail....................................... 10
　4. Sendero Esperanza Trail 13
　5. Hugh Norris Trail...................................... 16
　6. King Canyon Trail 20
　7. Brown Mountain.. 23
　8. David Yetman Trail..................................... 26

Santa Catalina Mountains
　9. Romero Canyon Trail................................... 32
　10. Pima Canyon Trail..................................... 35
　11. Finger Rock Spring.................................... 38
　12. Sabino Canyon Trail 41
　13. Seven Falls 44
　14. Butterfly Trail 47
　15. Aspen Trail... 50
　16. Wilderness of Rocks................................... 53

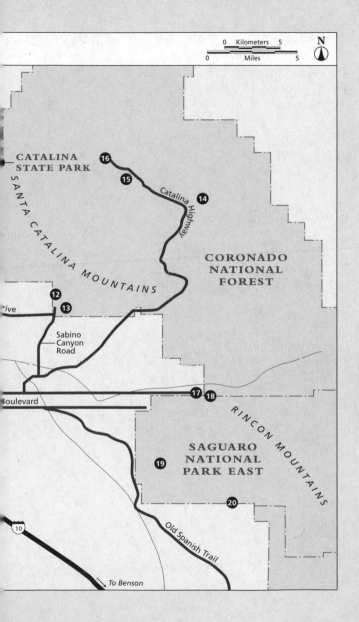

Rincon Mountains

17. Garwood Trail 59
18. Bridal Wreath Falls 62
19. Cactus Forest Trail 66
20. Ridge View Trail.. 70

Clubs and Trail Groups 73
About the Author 74

Acknowledgments

I would like to thank my many hiking companions down the years, who've put up with my incessant trail mapping and photography. Thanks to Duart Martin, for her support and encouragement. And finally, thanks to my editor at FalconGuides, Katie Benoit, for creating a polished book out of my rough manuscript. Thanks also to Melissa Baker for the excellent trail maps.

Introduction

Tucson residents and visitors are very lucky, living as they do in a historic city set in one of the most beautiful deserts in the world and surrounded by a dramatic mountain skyline. Within a few miles of the city, there are three mountain ranges—the Tucson Mountains, the Santa Catalina Mountains, and the Rincon Mountains. Each of these three ranges has its own unique characteristics, and each offers special hiking opportunities.

The Tucson Mountains are west of the city. This low desert mountain range, which reaches 4,662 feet at Wasson Peak, is largely protected within Saguaro National Park West and Tucson Mountain Park. Within the two parks are some of the finest examples of Sonoran Desert landscape in the Southwest, as well as large stands of giant saguaro cactus, the symbol of the Sonoran Desert.

At the north side of Tucson, the Santa Catalina Mountains are the highest of the three areas covered by this book, reaching 9,130 feet at Mount Lemmon. The Catalinas, as locals call this striking and complex mountain range, have a paved highway to the top of the mountain, providing easy access to campgrounds, trails, summer homes, rock climbing crags, and even a ski area (the southernmost in the country). Luckily for the hiker, much of this complex range south and west of the Catalina Highway is included in the Pusch Ridge Wilderness, which is traversed by an extensive trail system.

The Rincon Mountains, which lie at the east edge of the city, rise more than 5,600 feet from their base to the 8,612-foot summit at Mica Mountain. Because of this great elevation range, the Rincon Mountains feature four distinct life zones, ranging from desert scrub to fir-aspen forest. There are numerous isolated mountain ranges that reach similar elevations in southeastern Arizona, but the Rincon high country is one of the few that has no road access. The Rincons are the domain of the hiker, backpacker, and horseback rider. Saguaro National Park East includes most of the Rincon Mountains; the rest lies in the Coronado National Forest.

Millions of years ago, during the formation of the North American continent, the area that is now southern Arizona was stretched from east to west by crustal forces. Numerous north-tending fractures, or faults, formed as the rocks broke under the strain. Some of the resulting blocks sank to form the valleys, while others rose to form the mountains. As the faulting continues to lower the basins and raise the mountains, erosion from water flowing downhill tends to wear down the mountains and fill the valleys. The topography we see today reflects the fact that the faulting is still active enough to keep the mountains from being worn down to a flat plain.

Hazards

Dehydration
Even in the mountains, where the summer air is cool, dehydration is a serious concern. Because the humidity is usually very low, your body loses moisture insensibly. Carry and drink more water than is needed to quench your thirst, and eat high-energy snacks for fuel and to help keep your electrolytes in balance. Both these measures are necessary to prevent heat exhaustion, which can rapidly develop into life-threatening heatstroke.

Plants and Animals

Various plants and animals can pose hazards to hikers in the Arizona desert and mountains. Plants that are hazardous to the touch include poison ivy and stinging nettle. Spiny plants like cactus are easy to avoid. Never eat any plant unless you know what you are doing. Many common plants, especially mushrooms, are deadly.

Animals will normally leave you alone unless molested or provoked. Never feed wild animals, as they rapidly get used to the handouts and then will vigorously defend their new food source.

Rattlesnakes cause concern, but they can easily be avoided. They usually warn off intruders by rattling well before you reach striking range. Since rattlesnakes can strike no farther than half their body length, avoid placing your hands and feet in areas you cannot see, and walk several feet away from rock overhangs and shady ledges. Snakes prefer surfaces at about 80°F, so during hot weather they prefer the shade of bushes or rock overhangs and in cool weather will be found sunning themselves on open ground.

Arizona's Sonoran Desert is home to a venomous lizard, the Gila monster. This yellow, orange, red, and black lizard is about a foot and a half long and is unmistakable. Although these lizards are rare and protected by state law, if you do see one, don't be fooled by its torpid appearance. If molested, Gila monsters can bite very suddenly.

Mosquitoes are occasionally around in small numbers after snowmelt at the higher elevations. Spring rains can sometimes bring out a few mosquitoes in the desert. Because mosquitoes can transmit West Nile and other viruses, use repellent and sleep in a tent when they are present. DEET in various concentrations seems to be the most effective repellent.

Africanized bees, originally released in South America, have spread north and are now well established in the Arizona deserts. Avoid all concentrations of bees, especially hives and swarms. If attacked, drop your pack and run. Protect your eyes, and don't swat at the bees. Try to get into brush or dense foliage, which confuses the bees.

Old mines and prospects are common in these mountains. While hazardous areas are supposed to be signed and fenced, in practice this doesn't always happen; a few people ignore the warnings and get hurt or killed every year. Vertical shafts are a serious hazard, especially in brushy areas. Use a flashlight when walking through brushy areas at night off-trail, even around camp. Never approach the edge of a pit or shaft; the edges are often unstable or undercut, and there's no way to tell how deep the hole is. Stay out of horizontal shafts and mines in general. They are often unstable, there can be partially covered or hidden vertical shafts, and poisonous or radioactive gas may be present.

Weather

As you would expect in a desert region, the weather is stable for long periods. Even during winter, when storms drop snow on the high peaks and rain on the desert floor, long periods of clear weather are the rule rather than the exception. Desert hiking is especially fine during the winter, when the mountaintops may be snow covered. Spring and fall are normally dry and offer the best weather for hiking at all elevations. After wet winters, spring often brings fantastic displays of wildflowers to the desert. When the heat of summer blasts the desert, it is best to either hike early in the morning or retreat to the top of the Santa Catalinas. July through mid-September brings a second wet period, the North

American monsoon, an influx of seasonal moisture from the Gulf of Mexico. Summer mornings often dawn clear, but by noon towering cumulus clouds may form over the mountains and develop into massive thunderstorms. Plan summer hikes to be off exposed ridges and summits by noon to avoid the thunderstorm hazards of lightning, high wind, and hail.

The best source for up-to-date weather information is the National Weather Service in Tucson; their website is www.weather.gov/tucson. Commercial weather sources concentrate on urban areas and highway corridors, but by using the National Weather Service website, you can click on a map and get a specific point forecast for the trail you plan to hike. This is important because the weather in the high mountains is usually much different than the weather in the city.

Gear Every Hiker Should Carry

- Water
- Food
- Sunhat
- Sunscreen
- Sunglasses
- Durable hiking shoes or boots
- Synthetic fleece jacket or pullover
- Rain gear
- Printed map
- Compass
- First-aid kit
- Signal mirror
- Toilet paper and zippered plastic bag

Environmental Considerations

The desert is a fragile environment that deserves our utmost care and respect. Please adhere to some simple practices when hiking and camping in the desert.

Stay on the trail. Don't cut switchbacks. It takes more effort on your part and causes erosion.

Be careful with fires. Smokers should stop at a bare spot or rock ledge and then make certain all smoking materials are out before continuing. Due to fire hazard, it may be illegal to smoke while traveling. Never smoke or light any kind of fire on windy days or when the fire danger is high—wildfires can start easily and spread explosively.

Control your pet. Although dogs are allowed on some of the trails in this book, it is your responsibility to keep them from barking and bothering wildlife or other hikers. In national forests, dogs must be kept under control and on a leash when required.

Respect the environment. Don't cut live trees or plants of any kind, carve on trees or rocks, pick wildflowers, or build structures such as rock campfire rings.

Share the trail. Many of the trails in this book are open to horseback riders as well as hikers, and some are open to mountain bikers as well. Horses always have the right-of-way over hikers and cyclists, both of which should move off the trail downhill and remain still until the horses have passed. Talking quietly to the riders helps convince the horses that you are a person and not some weird monster with a hump on its back. Don't make sudden movements or noises.

Technically, hikers have the right-of-way over cyclists, but in practice it's more reasonable for hikers to step off the trail so as to avoid forcing the riders off-trail. On their part, cyclists should be courteous, always ride under control, and warn hikers of their approach.

Sanitation

A short walk in any popular recreation area will show you that few people seem to know how to answer the call of nature away from facilities. Leaving human feces unburied is a common but totally barbaric practice that spreads disease, including giardiasis. If facilities are available, always use them. In the backcountry, select a site at least 100 yards from streams, lakes, springs, and dry washes. Choose organic soils and avoid barren, sandy soil, if possible. Next, dig a small "cat-hole" about 6 inches down into the organic layer of the soil. (Some people carry a small plastic trowel for this purpose.) When finished, refill the hole, covering any toilet paper. (None of the areas covered by this book require toilet paper to be packed out.)

As far as trash goes, if you carried it in, you can also carry it out. Do not bury food or trash. Animals will always dig it up. Never feed wild creatures. They become dependent on human food, which can lead to unpleasant encounters and cause the animal to starve during the off-season.

Three Falcon Zero-Impact Principles:

- Leave with everything you brought.
- Leave no sign of your visit.
- Leave the landscape as you found it.

How to Use This Book

This book is divided into three sections, covering the Tucson Mountains, Santa Catalina Mountains, and Rincon Mountains.

Each hike in the book has a number and name. Some trails have more than one common name, and other hikes use more than one trail to complete a loop or otherwise create a more interesting route. In each case, I've attempted to name the hike for the best-known trail or feature. Each hike starts with a general description of the highlights and attractions. A summary of the hike follows, with at-a-glance information.

Distance: This is the total mileage of the hike. For out-and-back hikes, it includes the return mileage. Loop hikes include the total distance around the loop. Some loops may have an out-and-back section, or cherry stem. Distances were measured on digital topographic maps and may vary slightly from official mileages, but they are consistent within the book.

Approximate hiking time: This is based on an average hiker who is reasonably fit. More casual hikers should allow more time. The hiking time does not include time for lunch stops, wildlife viewing, photography, or other distractions. Plan on additional time for such activities. Groups should remember that the party travels at the speed of the slowest member.

Difficulty: All hikes in this book are rated easy or moderate. There are no strenuous or difficult hikes in the book, but sections of trails may be steep, rough, or otherwise more strenuous than the overall rating would indicate. Just about anyone should be able to do an easy hike. Moderate hikes require a bit of fitness, and beginners should allow extra time.

Trail surface: The type of tread you'll be walking on.

Best season: Although most hikes can be done any time of the year, this section lists the best season, when temperatures and weather are at their most enjoyable. Low-elevation hikes in the Tucson Mountains and the foothills of the Santa Catalina and Rincon Mountains are generally best hiked from fall through spring because of the extremely hot desert summers. During summer, higher-elevation hikes in the Santa Catalina Mountains are preferable. If you hike at low elevation during summer, get an early start and take plenty of water.

Water availability: Although day hikers should carry all the water they need, this section lists known water sources for emergency use. If possible, all water should be purified before use.

Other trail users: These may include equestrians and mountain bikers.

Canine compatibility: Dogs are not allowed on trails in Saguaro National Park. Dogs are generally allowed in the state parks and national forests but must be under voice control or on a leash. This is just common courtesy to other hikers, some of whom may have had bad experiences with dogs. If your dog barks or runs up to other hikers, even in a friendly way, your dog is not under control and you are giving dog owners a bad name. Also, carry plastic bags and clean up after your dog.

Fees and permits: Entrance fees are charged in both units of Saguaro National Park, at Catalina State Park, and at Picacho Peak State Park; fees also are charged at most campgrounds and at Sabino Canyon.

Maps: Each hike has a map showing the trail and any pertinent landmarks. Hikers wishing to explore further, or off-trail, should carry the US Geological Survey topographic maps as listed here. These are the most detailed maps for terrain and natural features, but they do not show all trails. USGS maps are available free in digital form from USGS and within smartphone apps and web-based mapping programs. I strongly recommend that you print a copy of your topo map, especially if hiking cross-country or in an unfamiliar area. Batteries never die on paper maps. Another alternative is the excellent recreation maps produced by National Geographic Maps under the Trails Illustrated line (www.natgeomaps.com).

Trail contacts: This section lists the name, address, phone number, and website of the managing agency. It's a good idea to contact the agency for up-to-date trail information before your hike.

Finding the trailhead: Since the Tucson metropolitan area is large, the trailhead directions start from the nearest national park or USDA Forest Service visitor center. The GPS coordinates for the trailhead are listed in latitude/longitude (lat/long) format.

The Hike: This is a narrative description of the hike route and attractions you'll find along the way. There are also descriptions of relevant natural or human history.

Miles and Directions: This table lists the key points, such as trail intersections, or turning points on a cross-country hike, by miles and tenths. You should be able to find the route with this table alone. The mileages in this book do not necessarily agree with distances found on trails signs, agency mileages, and other descriptions, because trail miles are measured by a variety of methods and personnel. All mileages in this book were carefully measured using digital topographic mapping software for accuracy and consistency.

Trail Finder

Best Hikes for Geology Lovers

7   Brown Mountain
11   Finger Rock Spring
13   Seven Falls
16   Wilderness of Rocks
18   Bridal Wreath Falls
20   Ridge View Trail

Best Hikes for Children

3   Signal Hill Trail
15   Aspen Trail
19   Cactus Forest Trail

Best Hikes for Dogs

14   Butterfly Trail
15   Aspen Trail
16   Wilderness of Rocks

Best Hikes for Great Views

1   Picacho Peak
3   Signal Hill Trail
5   Hugh Norris Trail
6   King Canyon Trail
7   Brown Mountain
9   Romero Canyon Trail
15   Aspen Trail
16   Wilderness of Rocks
20   Ridge View Trail

Best Hikes for Photographers

1   Picacho Peak
3   Signal Hill Trail
8   David Yetman Trail
12   Sabino Canyon Trail
13   Seven Falls
18   Bridal Wreath Falls
19   Cactus Forest Trail

Best Hikes for Canyons

6   King Canyon Trail
9   Romero Canyon Trail
10   Pima Canyon Trail
11   Finger Rock Spring
12   Sabino Canyon Trail
13   Seven Falls

Best Hikes for Nature Lovers

2   Picture Rocks Wash
3   Signal Hill Trail
8   David Yetman Trail
13   Seven Falls
15   Aspen Trail
18   Bridal Wreath Falls
19   Cactus Forest Trail

Legend

━━⑩━━	Interstate Highway
━━⑲⑴━━	US Highway
━━⑺⑺━━	State Highway
━━━━━	Local Road
━ ━ ━ ━	Unpaved Road
▬▬▬▬▬	Featured Route
- - - - - -	Trail
∿	River/Creek
⌇	Intermittent Stream
⬚	State Park/Forest
⬚	National Park/Forest
▲	Campground
╱	Dam
🅿	Parking
⌣	Pass/Gap
▲	Peak
🛆	Picnic Area
🛈	Ranger Station
🚌	Shuttle Bus Stop
×	Spot Elevation
⟁	Spring
○	Town
❶	Trailhead
✿	Viewpoint
❷	Visitor Center
≋	Waterfall

Tucson Mountains

Lying west of Tucson, Saguaro National Park West, together with Tucson Mountain Park, encompasses much of the Tucson Mountains. These desert mountains are the lowest of the three ranges covered in this book, culminating in 4,662-foot Wasson Peak. The foothills and south-facing slopes feature some of the best stands of saguaro cactus in the entire Sonoran Desert, while the higher ridges and peaks transition to desert grassland, where smaller cactus are more common. The range runs generally north to south but has several outlying portions. An extensive and popular network of trails covers much of the Tucson Mountains. All the hikes in this section are in the Tucson Mountains, except for Hike 1: Picacho Peak.

The Red Hills Visitor Center is a good place to start your visit to the Tucson Mountains. The visitor center has exhibits, books, and maps, and staff can answer your questions about hiking in the area. The visitor center is the starting point for the trailhead directions in this section, except for Hike 1: Picacho Peak.

If coming from the north, exit I-10 at Avra Valley Road, turn right, and drive 5.1 miles west to Sandario Road. Turn left and drive 8.9 miles, and then turn left onto Mile Wide Road. Drive east 1.7 miles, and then turn left onto Kinney Road and drive 0.9 mile to the Red Hills Visitor Center.

From central Tucson, leave I-10 at the Speedway Boulevard exit and drive 4.7 miles west on Speedway, where it becomes Gates Pass Road. Stay on Gates Pass Road over Gates Pass (Tucson Mountain Park lies south of the road; Saguaro National Park to the north) another 2.9 miles, and then turn right onto Kinney Road. Drive 4.7 miles northwest on Kinney Road to the Red Hills Visitor Center. Gates Pass Road is narrow and winding and not recommended for RVs and trailers.

From the south, exit I-19 onto Ajo Way and head west 5.1 miles, where you'll turn right onto Kinney Road. Kinney Road passes through Tucson Mountain Park and then enters Saguaro National Park. After 10.0 miles you'll arrive at the Red Hills Visitor Center.

1 Picacho Peak

Although this hike is well northwest of the Tucson Mountains, it should not be missed. It follows the Hunter Trail to the top of Picacho Peak, the spectacular rocky summit adjacent to I-10 northwest of Tucson.

Distance: 4.0 miles out and back
Approximate hiking time: 4 hours
Difficulty: Moderate due to elevation change
Trail surface: Dirt and rocks
Best season: Fall through spring
Water availability: None
Other trail users: None
Canine compatibility: Leashed dogs allowed

Fees and permits: Park entrance fee
Maps: USGS Newman Peak
Trail contacts: Picacho Peak State Park, PO Box 907, Eloy 85131; (520) 466-3183; http://azstateparks.com/Parks/PIPE/index.html

Finding the trailhead: From Tucson, drive 50 miles north on I-10 to the well-marked exit for Picacho Peak State Park. The trailhead is located in the southwest corner of the park's Barrett Loop, near the Saguaro Ramada. GPS: N32° 38.54925' / W111° 24.19612'

The Hike

In 1933 the Civilian Conservation Corps built a trail to the summit that now sees 10,000 or more hikers a year. In the early 1970s, an Explorer Scout Troop constructed a new trail to replace the lower half of the original CCC trail. At the junction with the Sunset Vista Trail, stay left and continue on the Hunter Trail. Frequent trail signs and steel-cable handrails show the way over the eastern headwall to the main saddle.

From the saddle, railroad-tie wooden steps, steel cables, wire mesh–enclosed catwalks, and gangplanks lead to the summit. On a clear day there are 100-mile views in all directions. Unfortunately, with each passing year, there is less of the natural desert landscape and more urban development surrounding the park.

Rising 1,500 vertical feet above the surrounding desert floor, 3,320-foot Picacho Peak is an isolated, 22-million-year-old volcanic mountain situated midway between the Gila River and Tucson. This is the site of Arizona's only Civil War battle. The Battle of Picacho Pass took place on April 15, 1862, lasted about an hour and a half, and cost the lives of four "Johnny Rebs" and three "Yanks." Petroglyphs abound

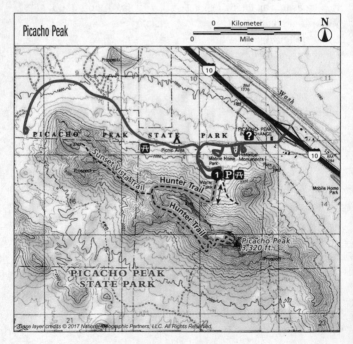

in the area, testifying that the prehistoric Hohokam were here long before the white man.

Miles and Directions

0.0 Leave the Picacho Peak Trailhead on the Hunter Trail.

0.8 The Sunset Vista Trail joins from the right; stay left on the Hunter Trail.

2.0 Reach the Summit of Picacho Peak; return the way you came.

4.0 Arrive back at the Picacho Peak Trailhead.

2 Picture Rocks Wash

This hike leads you through a beautiful saguaro cactus forest in Sonoran Desert hills, using the Ironwood Forest and Picture Rocks Wash Trails. These trails are in the northern portion of the Tucson Mountains, in Saguaro National Park West.

Distance: 5.4 miles out and back
Approximate hiking time: 3 hours
Difficulty: Easy
Trail surface: Dirt and rocks
Best season: Fall through spring
Water availability: None
Other trail users: Horses
Canine compatibility: Dogs not allowed

Fees and permits: Entrance fee
Maps: USGS Avra, Jaynes; National Geographic: Saguaro National Park
Trail contacts: Saguaro National Park, 3693 S. Old Spanish Rd., Tucson 85730; (520) 733-5158; www.nps.gov/sagu/index.htm

Finding the trailhead: From the Red Hills Visitor Center, turn right onto Kinney Road and drive 2.1 miles to Sandario Road. Turn right and continue north 3.7 miles, and then turn right onto Picture Rocks Road. Follow this road east 5.5 miles to the unsigned parking area on the left, just before the road goes over Contzen Pass. GPS: N32° 19.64940' / W111° 07.87436'

The Hike

This easy hike through rolling Sonoran Desert foothills starts out on the Cam-Boh Trail. Cross Picture Rocks Road and follow the trail down the wash. Almost immediately, the Ringtail Trail forks left; stay right on the Cam-Boh Trail, which parallels the nearby Picture Rocks Road. Next, turn left on the Ironwood Forest Trail, which heads south and climbs gradually through the low desert foothills.

You are walking through the Lower Sonoran life zone, characterized by saguaro, cholla, and barrel cactus; green-barked paloverde trees; and creosote bush. Watch for small saguaros nearly hidden in the shade of their nurse trees, usually paloverde. Paloverde trees have several adaptations to the hot, dry desert climate. Although the tree is seldom more than 10 feet high, its taproot can reach deep water 100 feet or more below the surface. Paloverdes carry on photosynthesis in their green bark (*paloverde* is Spanish for "green stick") most of the year. If the winter rains have been sufficient, paloverdes leaf out in spring, taking advantage of the temporary moisture to put on a spurt of growth. As soon as the weather turns dry and hot, the tree drops its leaves, greatly reducing the amount of moisture lost via transpiration. After wet winters, paloverdes are often covered with millions of tiny yellow or white flowers.

The Ironwood Forest Trail works its way into higher hills and finally climbs over a saddle and drops into Picture Rocks Wash, meeting the Picture Rocks Wash Trail. Turn right and continue past the Brittlebrush Trail, staying in the wash on the Picture Rocks Wash Trail to its end in the upper end of the wash.

Ironwood trees have, as the name implies, extremely hard wood. Popular with wood carvers, the wood is also in much demand as an especially long-burning firewood, as well as for fence posts. In many portions of the Sonoran Desert, the ironwood has nearly disappeared. It is protected here in Saguaro National Park, as well as in the new Ironwood Forest National Monument.

There is a recurring myth that all deserts are shaped by wind. Although some are, the North American deserts, including the Sonoran, are shaped and eroded primarily by water. As faulting activity lifted the Tucson Mountains, running water tore them down. This process continues today. Most erosion takes place during infrequent heavy rains, which usually occur during the late summer monsoon. Even though the ground is usually dry, it can't absorb heavy

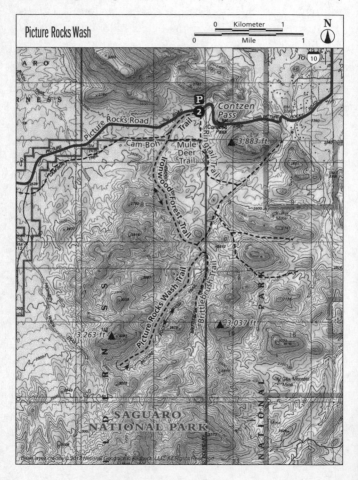

thunderstorm rains, which often fall at a rate of 2 inches per hour or more. The water runs off the bare ground between the widely spaced plants in sheets, carrying anything loose with it. The water quickly gathers into small drainages, which in turn lead into larger drainages and eventually into washes such as Picture Rocks Wash. Flowing water's ability to carry silt, sand, pebbles, and boulders increases rapidly as the velocity of the flow increases, so major floods carry a load of sand and rock. These floods, sometimes more debris than water, act like giant rasps to wear down the beds of the washes and tear away the banks. Look closely at nearly any dry wash and you can see the signs of the last flood: undercut banks, debris piled in the trees and brush next to the wash, and dried potholes.

Miles and Directions

0.0 Leave the trailhead and follow the wash downhill and across the road.

0.1 The Ringtail Trail joins from the left; stay right on the Cam-Boh Trail.

0.4 Turn left onto the Ironwood Forest Trail.

1.4 Turn right onto the Picture Rocks Wash Trail.

1.6 The Brittlebrush Trail comes in on the left; stay right on the Picture Rocks Wash Trail.

2.7 Trail ends in upper Picture Rocks Wash; return the way you came.

5.4 Arrive back at the trailhead.

3 Signal Hill Trail

The Signal Hill Trail is a short walk to a hill with a 360-degree view of the northern Tucson Mountains, as well as fine examples of ancient petroglyphs.

Distance: 0.4 mile out and back
Approximate hiking time: 0.5 hour
Difficulty: Easy
Trail surface: Dirt and rocks
Best season: Fall through spring
Water availability: None
Other trail users: None

Canine compatibility: Dogs not allowed
Fees and permits: Entrance fee
Maps: USGS Avra; National Geographic: Saguaro National Park
Trail contacts: Saguaro National Park, 3693 S. Old Spanish Rd., Tucson 85730; (520) 733-5158; www.nps.gov/sagu/index.htm

Finding the trailhead: From the Red Hills Visitor Center, turn right onto Kinney Road. After 2.1 miles, turn right onto Sandario Road. In just 0.2 mile, turn right onto Golden Gate Road; then drive 1.2 miles to Signal Hill Road and turn left. Continue 0.4 mile to the Signal Hill Picnic Area and park. GPS: N32° 17.38221' / N111° 12.52097'

The Hike

This very short trail leads to the top of a small hill with a fine collection of petroglyphs. There are two main types of rock art: pictographs, which are painted onto the rock, and petroglyphs such as these, which are pecked or carved into the rock. Although some people have the impression that petroglyphs are casual doodling, stone is actually a difficult medium to work, somewhat harder than doodling on a pad of paper. The ancient artists had to pick the site carefully.

They needed hard rocks with a solid coating of the dark desert varnish that forms after centuries of exposure to the relentless desert sun, and a location where the rocks would not be covered by floods or washed away. The care with which these people created their art is evident in its durability. How many modern artworks will last for centuries?

Looking around from Signal Hill, low though it is, your eye can rove over much of the Tucson Mountains. Apache Peak lies in the foreground to the east. To the southeast rises the long ridge that leads east to the highest portion of the range, culminating in 4,393-foot Amole Peak and 4,662-foot Wasson Peak. To the west lies the vast sweep of Avra

Valley, much of it overlaid with farmland and houses. North of Signal Hill, virtually at your feet, lies several square miles of desert plain that is in its natural state, part of the Saguaro Wilderness and Saguaro National Park.

In the distant north, look for a sharp, isolated peak—Picacho Peak, site of Arizona's only Civil War battle. *Picacho* means "peak" in Spanish, so the Anglicized name is somewhat redundant.

Many of the isolated desert mountains that you can see from this viewpoint are the remains of desert ranges that have been nearly eroded away. Early in their lives, fault-block mountains form a long, narrow, continuous range. As occasional heavy storms erode the mountains, debris is carried down the steep slopes to the foothills, and then out into the desert valleys along washes. Gradually the mountains are worn down; at the same time the valleys fill with this alluvial debris, burying the mountains in their own detritus, leaving isolated remnants of the mountains standing alone on the plains.

Miles and Directions

0.0 Leave the trailhead at Signal Hill Picnic Area and start up the Signal Hill Trail.

0.2 Arrive at the summit and the petroglyphs; return the way you came.

0.4 Arrive back at the trailhead at Signal Hill Picnic Area.

4 Sendero Esperanza Trail

This pleasant hike takes you through gorgeous saguaro forest to a saddle on the rugged Tucson Mountains. This point on the west ridge of Wasson Peak offers a great view of the deserts and mountains far to the west.

Distance: 3.0 miles out and back
Approximate hiking time: 2 hours
Difficulty: Moderate due to elevation gain
Trail surface: Dirt and rocks
Best season: Fall through spring
Water availability: None
Other trail users: Horses

Canine compatibility: Dogs not allowed
Fees and permits: Entrance fee
Maps: USGS Avra; National Geographic: Saguaro National Park
Trail contacts: Saguaro National Park, 3693 S. Old Spanish Rd., Tucson 85730; (520) 733-5158; www.nps.gov/sagu/index.htm

Finding the trailhead: From the Red Hills Visitor Center, turn right onto Kinney Road. After 2.1 miles, turn right onto Sandario Road. In just 0.2 mile, turn right onto Golden Gate Road, and then drive 3.8 miles to the Sendero Esperanza Trailhead, on the right. GPS: N32° 17.11846' / W111° 10.07798'

The Hike

This hike takes you across desert flats through fine stands of saguaro cactus. Look for holes in the saguaros, well above the ground, as you walk. Several different birds and animals make their home by hollowing out these holes. After the cactus dies, falls, and decays, you can sometimes find the intact nests, which are known as saguaro "boots."

The Sendero Esperanza Trail partially follows the route of an old road, as do many trails in the Tucson Mountains. These roads were usually built by miners and prospectors before the creation of the national park. The desert has attracted prospectors since the beginning of European settlement, and prospectors were often the first people to explore a desert area. Prospects are everywhere, usually just small holes in the ground where a prospector explored a likely-looking rock outcrop. Some prospect holes are deep enough to be dangerous, and they are sometimes partially hidden by brush. One

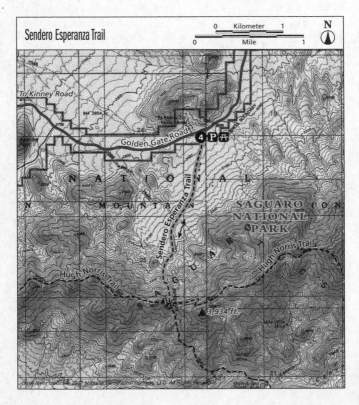

giveaway is the heaps of spoil, the dirt and rocks removed from the hole and piled nearby, though sometimes the spoil gets washed away in floods.

After a mile of gradual ascent, the Sendero Esperanza Trail climbs to meet the Hugh Norris Trail on the crest of the Tucson Mountains in a saddle. Views of the surrounding desert hills are great from this saddle.

Miles and Directions

0.0   Leave the Sendero Esperanza Trailhead and start on the Sendero Esperanza Trail.

1.5   Reach the Hugh Norris Trail at a saddle on the main ridge. Return the way you came.

3.0   Arrive back at the Sendero Esperanza Trailhead.

5 Hugh Norris Trail

This popular hike follows the main crest of the Tucson Mountains for an exceptionally scenic walk to the highest peak in the range.

Distance: 7.8 miles out and back
Approximate hiking time: 6 hours
Difficulty: Moderate due to elevation gain
Trail surface: Dirt and rocks
Best season: Fall through spring
Water availability: None
Other trail users: Horses
Canine compatibility: Dogs not allowed
Fees and permits: Entrance fee

Maps: USGS Avra; National Geographic: Saguaro National Park
Trail contacts: Saguaro National Park, 3693 S. Old Spanish Rd., Tucson 85730; (520) 733-5158; www.nps.gov/sagu/index.htm
Special considerations: During the hot summer months, plan your hike for early in the morning and carry plenty of water. The trail climbs more than 2,000 feet.

Finding the trailhead: From the Red Hills Visitor Center, turn right and drive northwest 1.7 miles on Kinney Road. Turn right onto Bajada Loop Drive (aka Hohokam Road) and continue 0.8 mile to the Hugh Norris Trailhead, on the right. GPS: N32° 16.27085' / W111° 12.25785'

The Hike

Named for a Tohono O'odham police chief, the Hugh Norris Trail starts from Bajada Loop Drive and climbs east up a small, unnamed canyon in the Tucson Mountains. A few switchbacks lead to a saddle, and after passing through another saddle, the trail climbs around the north side of a small peak. The trail soon gains the crest of the main ridge and more or less follows this ridge line east and down to a saddle, where the Sendero Esperanza Trail crosses. Continue east on the Hugh Norris Trail, which now resumes its steady climb along the ridge. You'll notice that the saguaro cactus starts to give way to high-desert grassland as you gain elevation, especially on the north-facing slopes. After you pass the south side of Amole Peak, a few steep switchbacks lead back to the main ridge and a trail junction. Here the Sweetwater Trail heads east; turn left (north) onto the Wasson Peak Trail and hike 0.2 mile to the summit. Wasson Peak is named for John Wasson, an early editor of the *Tucson Citizen*.

Your effort is rewarded with a 360-degree view of the Tucson Mountains, Avra Valley to the west, Tucson and the Santa Catalina and Rincon Mountains to the east, and in the distant south, the Santa Rita Mountains.

Saguaro cacti are extremely susceptible to subfreezing temperatures, which is why the Sonoran Desert is the only one of the four North American deserts that supports them. The Mojave, Great Basin, and Chihuahuan Deserts are all too cold. Even in the Sonoran Desert, the range of the saguaros is limited by the local climate. As you look around, you'll notice that saguaros march farther up south- and west-facing slopes than they do on north and east aspects. This is because north and east slopes get less heat from the sun, especially in winter, and subfreezing temperatures are both more common and more prolonged. Even a slight, short-term shift in the local climate will kill the most exposed, highest stands of saguaro.

On the other hand, as you gain elevation in the Tucson Mountains, the slopes become slightly wetter and not quite as hot as the lower slopes. This causes a transition to the Upper Sonoran life zone, which is just moist enough to allow some grasses to grow.

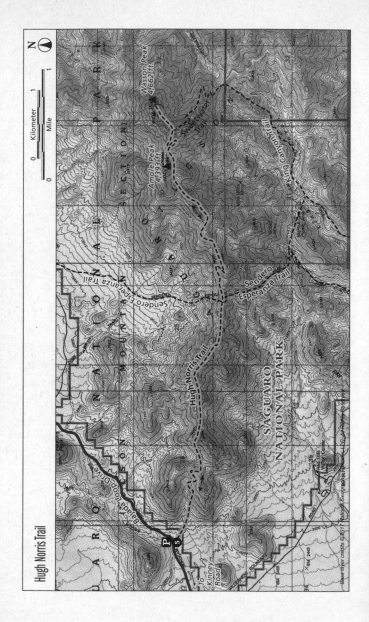

Hugh Norris Trail

Miles and Directions

0.0 Leave the Hugh Norris Trailhead and follow the Hugh Norris Trail east.

2.2 Cross the Sendero Esperanza Trail at a saddle and remain on the Hugh Norris Trail.

3.7 Turn left onto the Wasson Peak Trail.

3.9 Arrive at Wasson Peak; return the way you came.

7.8 Arrive back at the Hugh Norris Trailhead.

6 King Canyon Trail

This trail is an alternative route to popular Wasson Peak using the King Canyon and Sweetwater Trails. This hike takes you up the south slopes of the Tucson Mountains and then up the very scenic east ridge of Wasson Peak to the summit.

Distance: 6.0 miles out and back
Approximate hiking time: 4 hours
Difficulty: Moderate due to elevation gain
Trail surface: Dirt and rocks
Best season: Fall through spring
Water availability: None
Other trail users: Horses
Canine compatibility: Dogs not allowed
Fees and permits: Entrance fee

Maps: USGS Brown Mountain, Avra; National Geographic: Saguaro National Park
Trail contacts: Saguaro National Park, 3693 S. Old Spanish Rd., Tucson 85730; (520) 733-5158; www.nps.gov/sagu/index.htm
Special considerations: Carry plenty of water during the hot summer months. This trail climbs 1,700 feet.

Finding the trailhead: From the Red Hills Visitor Center, turn left onto Kinney Road and drive 1.9 miles to the King Canyon/Gould Mine Trailhead, which is a dirt parking lot on the left just before the Arizona Sonora Desert Museum. GPS: N32° 14.83159' / W111° 10.03364'

The Hike

Two trails leave the parking area; head northeast on the King Canyon Trail, an old mining road. In several places you can see elaborate cut stonework done during the construction of this road.

Occasionally a prospector actually discovered a valuable mineral deposit. In order to "prove the claim" and eventually acquire ownership of the public land containing the mineral deposit, a prospector had to develop the find and show that the deposit was rich enough to be profitably mined. This usually involved constructing a road, or at least a good trail, to the claim. Luckily for the future national park and wilderness, most mining claims in the Tucson Mountains were unprofitable.

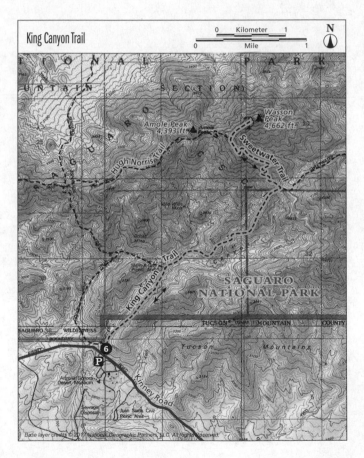

The USGS topographic map of this area shows the Mile Wide Mine on the slopes to the east, and you can see the scars of several old roads built to reach mines on the steep hillsides. Although initial reports in 1916 were optimistic that the mines in the head of King Canyon would be major copper producers, little copper was produced, and the mine works were eventually abandoned.

The trail continues up King Canyon, and after 0.9 mile passes the Mam-A-Gah Picnic Area and the Sendero Esperanza Trail. Stay right on the King Canyon Trail as it climbs through a Sonoran Desert basin studded with saguaro and cholla cactus. Shortly, the trail begins a steep climb up a ridge. When the King Canyon Trail reaches a saddle on the main crest of the Tucson Mountains, it ends at the Sweetwater Trail. Here you can look down a canyon to the northeast and see part of the Tucson valley and the Santa Catalina Mountains.

Turn left and follow the Sweetwater Trail up a series of switchbacks that climb the steep ridge to the west. You'll see several marked and fenced old mine shafts next to the trail along this section. About 0.6 mile of this steep ascent leads to the junction of the Hugh Norris and Wasson Peak Trails. Turn right onto the Wasson Peak Trail and hike 0.2 mile to the summit.

Miles and Directions

0.0   Leave the King Canyon Trailhead on the King Canyon Trail.

0.9   Reach the junction with the Sendero Esperanza Trail and the Mam-A-Gah Picnic Area; stay right on the King Canyon Trail.

2.2   Reach the main ridge and turn left onto the Sweetwater Trail.

2.8   Turn right on the Wasson Peak Trail.

3.0   Arrive at Wasson Peak; return the way you came.

6.0   Arrive back at the King Canyon Trailhead.

7 Brown Mountain

Brown Mountain is an easy hike, located in Tucson Mountain Park, along the top of a desert ridge with 50-mile views. Although the mountain is small, it is a classic sample of the delightful mix of vegetation that makes the Sonoran Desert the lushest of the four North American deserts.

Distance: 3.0 miles out and back
Approximate hiking time: 2 hours
Difficulty: Easy
Trail surface: Dirt and rocks
Best season: Fall through spring
Water availability: None
Other trail users: Horses
Canine compatibility: Dogs not allowed
Fees and permits: Entrance fee
Maps: USGS Brown Mountain; National Geographic: Saguaro National Park

Trail contacts: Pima County Natural Resources, Parks, and Recreation Department, 3500 W. River Rd., Tucson 86741; (520) 724-5000; www.pima.gov/nrpr/parks/tucs_mtpk/index.htm
Special considerations: During the hot summer months, plan to hike early in the day and carry plenty of water.

Finding the trailhead: From the Red Hills Visitor Center, turn left onto Kinney Road and drive 3.5 miles to the unsigned trailhead on the right. This parking area is past the Arizona Sonora Desert Museum but just before the Brown Mountain Picnic Area. GPS: N32° 13.92327' / W111° 08.76150'

The Hike

Head south toward the east end of Brown Mountain, staying right at two unsigned trail junctions. After the second junction, the trail turns sharply northwest and starts to climb the east slopes of Brown Mountain. As you climb, the views expand. Visible to the southeast, at the foot of the mountain, is the Brown Mountain Picnic Area and, beyond it, Gilbert Ray Campground. Once on the ridge crest, the trail more or less follows the crest northwest. There is a great variety of saguaros along the trail, including a number of young saguaros only about 5 or 6 feet tall.

The Brown Mountain Trail continues to the northwest end of the ridge, which is a good turnaround point. (From

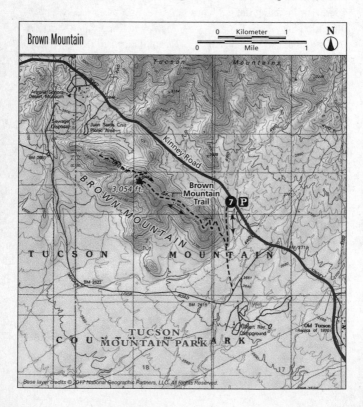

here, the trail descends to the Juan Santa Cruz Picnic Area.) Brown Mountain is a detached, outlying ridge and gives you a panoramic view of the Tucson Mountains, as well as the sweep of Avra Valley to the west and the Baboquivari Mountains to the southwest. The Baboquivari Mountains are marked by two prominent and unmistakable summits. Monolithic Baboquivari Peak, toward the south end of the range, is one of the few Arizona summits that require rock-climbing skills and equipment. Kitt Peak, at the north end of the range, is the site of a large solar and stellar observatory. The telescope domes are easily spotted from more than 30 miles away.

North of the turnaround point, partly blocked by the northwestern end of Brown Mountain, you can see the Arizona–Sonora Desert Museum, a place worth visiting if you wish to learn more about the plants and animals of the Sonoran Desert.

Brown Mountain is named for Cornelius Brown, who helped create Tucson Mountain Park in 1929 and is regarded as the father of the park.

Miles and Directions

0.0 Leave the trailhead on the Brown Mountain Trail.

0.3 Pass an unsigned trail junction; stay right.

0.4 Pass a second unsigned trail junction; stay right.

1.5 Arrive at the turnaround point at the north end of Brown Mountain; return the way you came.

3.0 Arrive back at the starting trailhead.

8 David Yetman Trail

The David Yetman Trail passes through varied Sonoran Desert terrain at the southern end of the Tucson Mountains. The trail is in Tucson Mountain Park.

Distance: 5.8 miles with shuttle
Approximate hiking time: 4 hours
Difficulty: Moderate due to length and elevation change
Trail surface: Dirt and rocks
Best season: Fall through spring
Water availability: None
Other trail users: Horses
Canine compatibility: Dogs not allowed
Fees and permits: Entrance fee

Maps: USGS Cat Mountain, Brown Mountain; National Geographic: Saguaro National Park
Trail contacts: Pima County Natural Resources, Parks, and Recreation Department, 3500 W. River Rd., Tucson 86741; (520) 724-5000; www.pima.gov/nrpr/parks/tucs_mtpk/index.htm
Special considerations: During the hot summer months, plan to hike early in the day and carry plenty of water.

Finding the trailhead: From the Red Hills Visitor Center, turn left onto Kinney Road. Drive 4.7 miles and then turn left onto Gates Pass Road. Drive another 1.7 miles and then turn right into the Yetman Trailhead (West). To reach the Yetman Trailhead (East) (GPS: N32° 13.4115' / W111° 3.73662'), turn right onto Gates Pass Road. After 2.9 miles, turn right onto Camino del Oeste and drive 0.9 mile south to the end of the road. GPS: N32° 13.05702' / W111° 06.20174'

The Hike

This hike requires a car shuttle; you'll need to drop a second vehicle at Yetman Trailhead (East). Starting from the west trailhead, the David Yetman Trail heads southeast toward a pass. At the pass, the Golden Gate Trail merges from the right; stay left and follow the Yetman Trail down to the flats at the base of Golden Gate Mountain. Here the Yetman Link Trail forks right; stay left on the Yetman Trail and follow it east. Climbing into the Tucson Mountains once again, the Yetman Trail crosses another unnamed pass and then descends a canyon to the east. After emerging into a broad desert basin, the Yetman Trail meets the Kennedy Park Trail; stay left on the Yetman Trail. Stay left at the junction with the Starr Pass Trail also, and follow the Yetman Trail north past the Starr

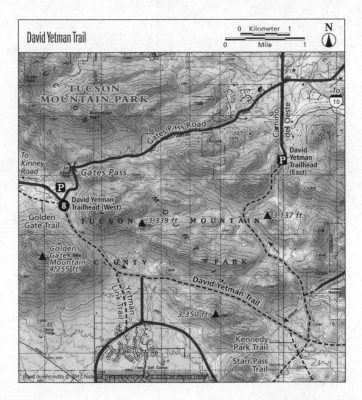

Pass Trailhead (East) and over a low pass. Now the Yetman Trail descends generally north, following a drainage system the remaining distance to Yetman Trailhead (East). This is the end of the hike if you left a shuttle vehicle here; otherwise, return the way you came.

The trail was named for David Yetman, who served on the Pima County Board of Supervisors from 1977 to 1988. Yetman was a strong defender of the environment, and the trail was named to honor him after his retirement.

Creosote bush, which is common in the Sonoran Desert, is an outstanding example of the extreme methods desert plants use to survive drought. During dry periods, the bush sheds its mature leaves as well as whole twigs and branches, retaining only the new leaves. These leaves can lose well over half their water and still survive. By comparison, humans are seriously ill after a water loss of only 10 percent.

Barrel cactus uses another strategy to survive in the desert. Rather than economizing on water during dry periods as the creosote bush does, the barrel cactus uses a widespread but shallow root system to rapidly collect groundwater after a rain. It then stores the moisture in the fleshy interior of the plant. Protecting this succulent interior is a nest of curved, overlapping, and very sharp spines. Desert lore has it that a thirsty traveler can break open a barrel cactus and dip out a cool drink. In reality, all you'll find is a bitter green core—after getting past the cactus's formidable defenses.

Miles and Directions

0.0 Leave the Yetman Trailhead (West) on the David Yetman Trail.

0.4 Pass the Golden Gate Trail junction; stay left on the David Yetman Trail.

1.1 Pass the Yetman Link Trail junction; stay left on the David Yetman Trail.

3.1 Pass the Kennedy Park Trail junction; stay left on the David Yetman Trail.

3.3 Pass the Starr Pass Trail turnoff; stay left on the David Yetman Trail.

3.8 Pass the Starr Pass Trailhead (East); stay left on the David Yetman Trail.

5.8 Arrive at Yetman Trailhead (East).

Santa Catalina Mountains

Rising to the north and east of Tucson, the Santa Catalina Mountains are the largest, highest, and most complex of the three mountain ranges next to Tucson. Elevations range from 2,700 feet at the base of the mountain to 9,130-foot Mount Lemmon, so, like the Rincon Mountains, the Catalinas encompass four distinct life zones from Lower Sonoran cactus and scrub to the Canadian mixed conifer and aspen on the summits and northeast slopes.

The steep ridges and rugged peaks rising from the desert floor and forming the northern skyline of Tucson are not actually the highest portion of the mountains but almost a separate range divided from the higher Mount Lemmon area by Sabino and Romero Canyons. Known locally as the Front Range, these deep canyons and rocky peaks are part of the Pusch Ridge Wilderness and are accessible only by trail.

Catalina State Park lies along the Canada del Oro at the west side of the range and provides access to several Catalina trailheads. In addition, the park has a trail system of its own, as well as picnic areas and a campground.

A ridge running southeast from Mount Lemmon forms the high crest of the Santa Catalinas, including several summits above 8,000 feet. In contrast to the rocky peaks of the Front Range, the crest area is relatively gentle. The Catalina Highway takes advantage of this terrain to more or less follow the crest to Mount Lemmon and provides easy access to the upper part of the mountain.

West and south of the Catalina Highway, canyons drop into more rugged country, such as the Wilderness of Rocks, much of which is in the northern and eastern portion of the Pusch Ridge Wilderness.

The Sabino Canyon Visitor Center, on the north side of Tucson, is a good place to visit before your hike, even if you're starting from another Santa Catalina trailhead. The visitor center has maps, books, and exhibits on the area, and staff can answer questions about current hiking conditions.

To reach the Sabino Canyon Visitor Center from I-10 north, exit at Ina Road and head east. After 5.6 miles, turn right onto Skyline Drive. In 3.2 miles stay right as the main road becomes Sunrise Drive. Continue east 6.4 miles to Sabino Canyon Road, turn left, then immediately right into the Sabino Canyon parking lot. There is a fee for parking here.

To reach the Sabino Canyon Visitor Center from Tucson, head north on Sabino Canyon Road. Just after Sunrise Drive, turn right into the Sabino Canyon parking lot.

9 Romero Canyon Trail

This hike leads to a collection of popular seasonal pools in Romero Canyon, starting from Catalina State Park and heading into the Pusch Ridge Wilderness in the Coronado National Forest.

Distance: 4.6 miles out and back

Approximate hiking time: 4 hours

Difficulty: Moderate due to distance and elevation change

Trail surface: Dirt and rocks

Best season: Fall through spring

Water availability: None

Other trail users: Horses

Canine compatibility: Dogs not allowed

Fees and permits: Entrance fee

Maps: USGS Oro Valley, Mount Lemmon; USFS: Coronado National Forest, Santa Catalina Ranger District

Trail contacts: Catalina State Park, PO Box 36986, Tucson 85740; (520) 628-5798; https://azstateparks.com; Coronado National Forest, Santa Catalina Ranger District, 5700 N. Sabino Canyon Rd., Tucson 85750; (520) 749-8700; www.fs.fed.us/r3/coronado/

Special considerations: Carry plenty of water during the hot summer months, and hike early in the day.

Finding the trailhead: From Sabino Canyon Visitor Center, turn left onto Sabino Canyon Road and then immediately right onto Sunrise Drive. After 6.4 miles, Sunrise becomes Skyline Drive; continue west another 1.9 miles, and then turn left onto Ina Road. After 1.7 miles, turn right onto Oracle Road (AZ 77). Continue north 6.2 miles, and then turn right into Catalina State Park. Drive 1.8 miles on the main park road to the Romero Canyon Trailhead, on the left. GPS: N32° 25.55245' / W110° 54.44585'

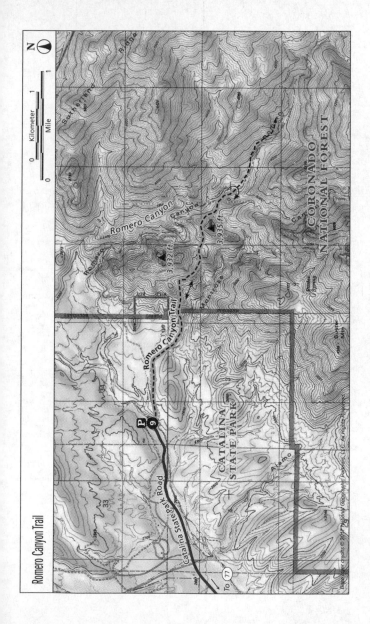

Romero Canyon Trail

The Hike

From the trailhead, cross the road and follow the broad trail across normally dry Canada del Oro. The hiking is easy with great views of the Front Range until you reach the base of the mountains, where the Romero Canyon Trail starts to climb in earnest. After climbing for a shorter distance than you expect, the trail turns southeast and contours through a saddle before descending into Romero Canyon. Seasonal pools of water along this section of Romero Canyon are known as Romero Pools. Spring is the best time to find water at this popular spot.

Seasonal pools such as these tend to occur in deep canyons where the additional shade helps keep the water from evaporating. In desert mountain ranges, such temporary pools are important water sources for wildlife, which may come from miles around. Hikers can use the water as well but should observe a few commonsense courtesies. Take only the water you need, and use it sparingly for all purposes except drinking. Never bathe in a pool or pollute it with soap or food scraps. Others will need the water. Avoid camping nearby, as your presence will scare away the animals that normally come to drink during the night. Finally, all desert water should be purified before drinking or cooking with it.

Miles and Directions

0.0 Leave the Romero Canyon Trailhead on the Romero Canyon Trail.

1.1 Reach the foothills and start climbing.

2.3 Arrive at Romero Canyon; return the way you came.

4.6 Arrive back at Romero Canyon Trailhead.

10 Pima Canyon Trail

This scenic route takes you into the rugged Pusch Ridge Wilderness, in the Front Range of the Santa Catalina Mountains. Although the hike starts in the outskirts of Tucson, which has now spread right to the base of the mountains, a few minutes' walking takes you from the sights and sounds of the city into a wilderness canyon.

Distance: 4.0 miles out and back
Approximate hiking time: 3 hours
Difficulty: Easy
Trail surface: Dirt and rocks
Best season: Fall through spring
Water availability: None
Other trail users: Horses
Canine compatibility: Dogs not allowed
Fees and permits: None
Maps: USGS Oro Valley, Tucson North; USFS: Pusch Ridge Wilderness

Trail contacts: Coronado National Forest, Santa Catalina Ranger District, 5700 N. Sabino Canyon Rd., Tucson 85750; (520) 749-8700; www.fs.fed.us/ r3/coronado/
Special considerations: Carry plenty of water during the hot summer months, and hike early in the day.

Finding the trailhead: From Sabino Canyon Visitor Center, turn left onto Sabino Canyon Road and then immediately right onto Sunrise Drive. After 6.4 miles, Sunrise becomes Skyline Drive; continue west another 1.9 miles, and then turn left onto Ina Road. After 0.7 mile, turn right onto Christie Drive. Continue north and northeast 1.4 miles, and then turn right and drive 0.2 mile to the Pima Canyon Trailhead. GPS: N32° 21.21833' / W110° 57.10939'

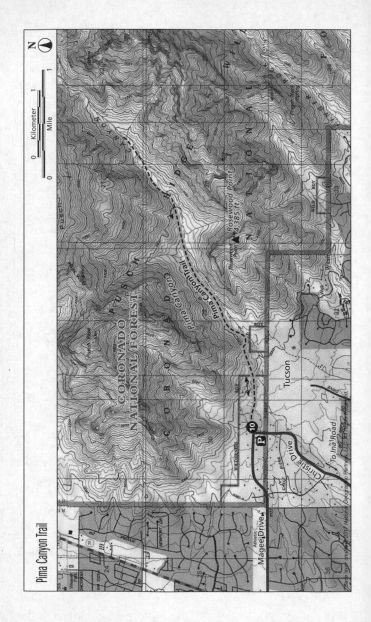

The Hike

The first section of the Pima Canyon Trail is on private land and is closely bordered by fences; please stay on the trail. After the trail enters the national forest and the Pusch Ridge Wilderness, it more or less follows the bottom of Pima Canyon as the canyon climbs northeast into the Front Range. Lower Pima Canyon is in the Lower Sonoran life zone, marked by saguaro, prickly pear, cholla, and barrel cactus; mesquite bushes; catclaw; and paloverde trees.

During the spring after snowmelt, the creek is often running, and later in the year there will still be seasonal pools, which are popular destinations during the hot months.

At first you'll have views of Tucson and the Santa Rita Mountains to the south, but as you continue the ascent of Pima Canyon past Rosewood Point, the view becomes blocked by the twists and turns of the canyon. In about 2 miles of hiking, you've left the city behind, out of sight and hearing, and have entered remote wilderness. At this point the trail becomes fainter and starts to climb more steeply into the head of Pima Canyon. This is the turnaround point for the hike.

Those wishing for a longer hike can continue up the Pima Canyon Trail to Pima Saddle and beyond. See *A FalconGuide to Saguaro National Park and the Santa Catalina Mountains* for details.

Miles and Directions

0.0 Start from the Pima Canyon Trailhead on the Pima Canyon Trail.

2.0 At this approximate distance, the Pima Canyon Trail becomes fainter; return the way you came.

4.0 Arrive back at the Pima Canyon Trailhead.

11 Finger Rock Spring

This hike uses the Finger Rock Canyon Trail to reach a seasonal spring in the Pusch Ridge Wilderness. The outing is especially enjoyable during or just after a wet winter, when a seasonal stream fills the normally dry wash.

Distance: 2.0 miles out and back
Approximate hiking time: 2 hours
Difficulty: Easy
Trail surface: Dirt and rocks
Best season: Fall through spring
Water availability: None
Other trail users: Horses
Canine compatibility: Dogs not allowed
Fees and permits: None
Maps: USGS Oro Valley, Tucson North; USFS: Pusch Ridge Wilderness

Trail contacts: Coronado National Forest, Santa Catalina Ranger District, 5700 N. Sabino Canyon Rd., Tucson 85750; (520) 749-8700; www.fs.fed.us/r3/coronado/
Special considerations: Carry plenty of water during the hot summer months, and hike early in the day.

Finding the trailhead: From Sabino Canyon Visitor Center, turn left onto Sabino Canyon Road and then immediately right onto Sunrise Drive. After 4.3 miles, turn right onto Swan Drive. Drive north 1.0 mile and turn left onto Skyline Drive; drive 1.0 mile west, and then turn right onto Alvernon Way. Continue north 0.9 mile to the Finger Rock Trailhead. GPS: N32° 20.24754' / W110° 54.62914'

The Hike

From the Finger Rock Trailhead, walk a few feet north up the road to the Finger Rock Canyon Trail, which heads north along the national forest boundary into the mouth of

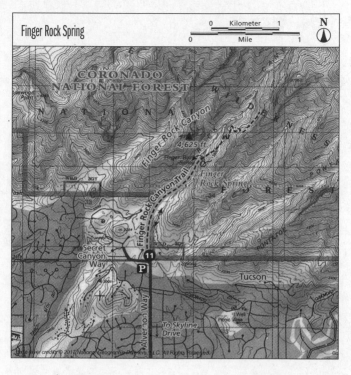

spectacular Finger Rock Canyon. The trail climbs the gentle slopes at the mouth of the canyon through typical Lower Sonoran vegetation: catclaw, mesquite, and saguaro and cholla cactus. Once in Finger Rock Canyon, the trail turns northeast and generally follows the bed of the canyon, passing seasonal Finger Rock Spring and seasonal pools along the way. This idyllic spot is the destination for our hike.

Beyond the spring, the Finger Rock Canyon Trail leaves the bed and climbs steeply to the head of the canyon. For details, see *A FalconGuide to Saguaro National Park and the Santa Catalina Mountains*.

Miles and Directions

0.0 Leave the Finger Rock Trailhead on the Finger Rock Canyon Trail.

1.0 Arrive at Finger Rock Spring, the destination for the hike; return the way you came.

2.0 Arrive back at the Finger Rock Trailhead.

12 Sabino Canyon Trail

This is a dramatic hike up Sabino Canyon and its West Fork to Hutch's Pool in the Front Range of the Santa Catalina Mountains and the Pusch Ridge Wilderness. The pools are a popular seasonal destination and are most likely to have water in spring or early summer after a wet winter.

Distance: 7.4 miles out and back
Approximate hiking time: 5 hours
Difficulty: Moderate due to elevation gain
Trail surface: Dirt and rocks
Best season: Fall through spring
Water availability: None
Other trail users: Horses
Canine compatibility: Dogs not allowed
Fees and permits: None

Maps: USGS Sabino Canyon, Mount Lemmon; USFS: Pusch Ridge Wilderness
Trail contacts: Coronado National Forest, Santa Catalina Ranger District, 5700 N. Sabino Canyon Rd., Tucson 85750; (520) 749-8700; www.fs.fed.us/r3/coronado/
Special considerations: During the hot summer months, plan your hike for early in the morning and carry plenty of water.

Finding the trailhead: To reach the Sabino Canyon Visitor Center from I-10 north, exit at Ina Road and head east. After 5.6 miles, turn right onto Skyline Drive. In 3.2 miles, stay right as the main road becomes Sunrise Drive. Continue east 6.4 miles to Sabino Canyon Road; turn left and then immediately right into the Sabino Canyon parking lot. There is a fee for parking here. GPS: N32° 18.60516' / W110° 49.37433'

To reach the Sabino Canyon Visitor Center from Tucson, head north on Sabino Canyon Road. Just after Sunrise Drive, turn right into the Sabino Canyon parking lot.

From Sabino Canyon Visitor Center, take the Sabino Canyon Shuttle 3.6 miles to the last stop in Sabino Canyon.

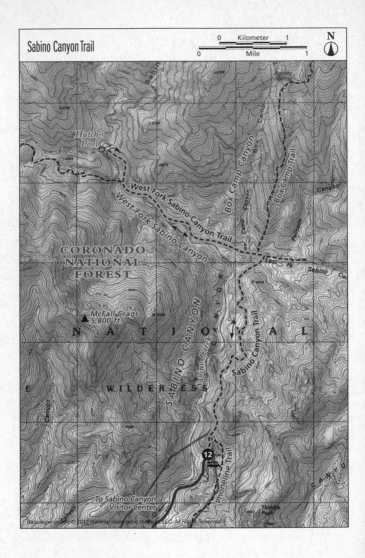

0   Kilometer   1

0   Mile   1

N

Sabino

6670

Apache
Spring

5740

Hutch's
Pool
4293

Box Camp Canyon

Box Camp Trail

West Fork Sabino Canyon Trail

West Fork Sabino Canyon

Canyon

CORONADO
NATIONAL
FOREST

East Fk.

Sabino Cr.

Sabino Can

R. Fork

6510

McFall Crags
5,800 ft.
5208

N   A   T   I   O   N   A   L

SABINO CANYON

Sabino Creek

Sabino Canyon Trail

E   WILDERNESS

Canyon

4700

12
Seven
Falls

Phoneline Trail

CANYO

To Sabino Canyon
Visitor Center

Thimble
Peak

The Hike

From the last shuttle stop in Sabino Canyon, hike north on the Sabino Canyon Trail, which climbs 0.1 mile to meet the Phoneline Trail. Stay left and follow the Sabino Canyon Trail north along the east side of Sabino Canyon to Sabino Basin. Sabino Basin, the confluence of the East and West Forks of Sabino Canyon, is a popular camp spot and the start of several trails that head into the Santa Catalina high country to the north.

In Sabino Basin, turn left onto the West Fork Sabino Canyon Trail. After just 0.1 mile, the Box Camp Trail goes right; stay left. Follow the West Fork Sabino Canyon Trail 2.5 miles west, until it veers left away from the bed of the canyon. Turn right onto an unmarked, informal trail and hike 0.1 mile up the West Fork to Hutch's Pool.

Miles and Directions

0.0 Leave the Sabino Canyon Trailhead on the Sabino Canyon Trail.

1.7 Turn left onto the West Fork Sabino Canyon Trail and follow it west up the West Fork of Sabino Canyon.

1.8 Pass the junction with the Box Camp Trail; stay left on the West Fork Sabino Canyon Trail.

3.3 Leave the West Fork Sabino Canyon Trail and turn right onto an unmarked trail.

3.7 Arrive at Hutch's Pool; return the way you came.

7.4 Arrive back at Sabino Canyon Trailhead.

13 Seven Falls

This walk leads to famous Seven Falls, a series of seasonal cascades in Bear Canyon, which uses the Bear Canyon Trail in the Pusch Ridge Wilderness. As with other seasonal streams in the Santa Catalina Mountains, the falls will be at their best in spring after a wet winter.

Distance: 4.0 miles out and back
Approximate hiking time: 5 hours
Difficulty: Easy
Trail surface: Dirt and rocks
Best season: Fall through spring
Water availability: None
Other trail users: Horses
Canine compatibility: Dogs not allowed
Fees and permits: None
Maps: USGS Sabino Canyon; USFS: Pusch Ridge Wilderness

Trail contacts: Coronado National Forest, Santa Catalina Ranger District, 5700 N. Sabino Canyon Rd., Tucson 85750; (520) 749-8700; www.fs.fed.us/r3/coronado/
Special considerations: During the hot summer months, plan your hike for early in the morning and carry plenty of water.

Finding the trailhead: To reach the Sabino Canyon Visitor Center from I-10 north, exit at Ina Road and head east. After 5.6 miles, turn right onto Skyline Drive. In 3.2 miles, stay right as the main road becomes Sunrise Drive. Continue east 6.4 miles to Sabino Canyon Road; turn left and then immediately right into the Sabino Canyon parking lot. There is a fee for parking here. GPS: N32° 18.60516' / W110° 49.37433'

To reach the Sabino Canyon Visitor Center from Tucson, head north on Sabino Canyon Road. Just after Sunrise Drive, turn right into the Sabino Canyon parking lot.

From Sabino Canyon Visitor Center, take the Bear Canyon Shuttle 2.5 miles to the Bear Canyon Trailhead at the end of the road.

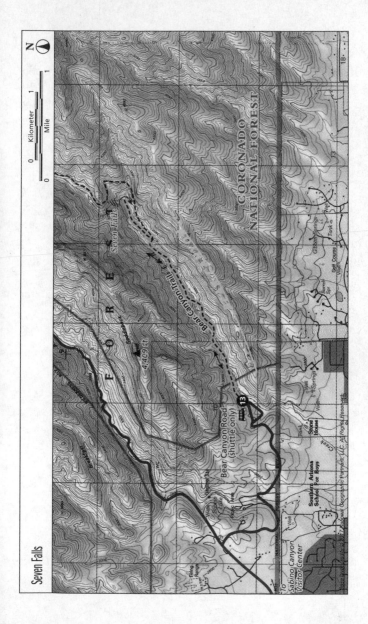

Seven Falls

The Hike

The extremely popular Bear Canyon Trail heads northeast up rugged Bear Canyon, crossing the seasonal creek numerous times. These crossings may be impossible during heavy spring runoff or after heavy late-summer thunderstorms. About 3.0 miles up the canyon, the trail switchbacks up the eastern wall and then gradually returns to the streambed. Where the canyon abruptly turns northwest, the trail climbs well above the canyon floor to avoid a series of cascades known locally as the Seven Falls. To explore the falls, leave the trail at the start of this climb and follow the streambed upstream. The falls are at their best after the spring snowmelt, which is usually late March or into April. Late-summer thunderstorms can also send large amounts of water through the canyon.

The falls are a popular spot and are heavily used. Be extra careful with litter, and be certain you pack everything out.

Miles and Directions

0.0 Leave the Bear Canyon Trailhead on the Bear Canyon Trail.

2.0 Arrive at Seven Falls; return the way you came.

4.0 Arrive back at Bear Canyon Trailhead.

14 Butterfly Trail

This is a cool hike through pine, fir, and aspen forest high on the northeast slopes of the Santa Catalina Mountains. It offers a welcome respite from the desert heat and is also pleasant in the fall, when the aspens and other deciduous plants are changing color.

Distance: 6.2 miles with shuttle
Approximate hiking time: 4 hours
Difficulty: Moderate due to distance and elevation change
Trail surface: Dirt and rocks
Best season: Spring through fall
Water availability: None
Other trail users: Horses
Canine compatibility: Dogs allowed on leash

Fees and permits: None
Maps: USGS Mount Bigelow; USFS: Pusch Ridge Wilderness
Trail contacts: Coronado National Forest, Santa Catalina Ranger District, 5700 N. Sabino Canyon Rd., Tucson 85750; (520) 749-8700; www.fs.fed.us/r3/coronado/

Finding the trailhead: From the Sabino Canyon Visitor Center, turn left onto Sabino Canyon Road; drive south 4.4 miles, and then turn left onto Tanque Verde Road. Drive east 2.6 miles, and then turn left onto Catalina Highway. Stay on the Catalina Highway (a fee is required, payable at the entrance station a few miles into the mountains) 33.0 miles to the Butterfly Trailhead, on the right. To reach the north trailhead (GPS: N33° 26.91018' / W110° 44.24622'), continue 4.6 miles on the Catalina Highway, and then turn right onto Old Mount Lemmon Road. Drive 3.0 miles on this dirt road to the Crystal Spring Trailhead, on the right. GPS: N32° 24.64049' / W110° 42.92370'

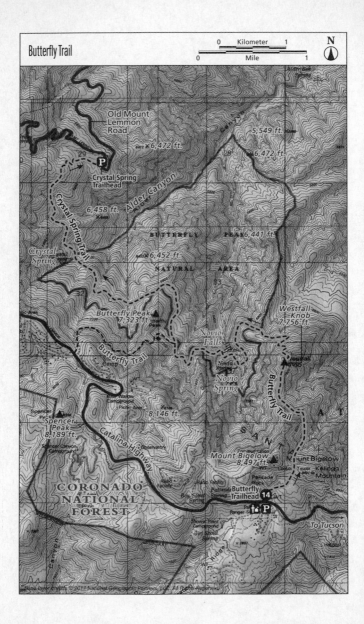

The Hike

The Butterfly Trail first heads northeast and climbs over the saddle between Mount Bigelow and Kellogg Peak, then swings north and descends along an east-facing slope. After passing over Westfall Knob, the trail descends along the ridge in a series of switchbacks and then turns west and contours into a canyon. When the Butterfly Trail crosses the main drainage, watch for Novio Spring, above the trail. There is also a seasonal waterfall in the drainage below the trail. This spot makes a good destination for an out-and-back hike.

Beyond Novio Spring, the Butterfly Trail continues to descend until it meets the Crystal Spring Trail southeast of Butterfly Peak. At this junction, the Butterfly Trail goes left; turn right onto the Crystal Spring Trail, which swings around the north slopes of Butterfly Peak and then crosses into the Alder Creek drainage. Crystal Spring is located in the main fork of Alder Creek. After Crystal Spring, the trail climbs north along the east-facing slopes of Alder Canyon before descending steeply to end at the Old Mount Lemmon Road and the north trailhead.

Miles and Directions

0.0 Leave the Butterfly Trailhead on the Butterfly Trail.

0.4 Pass through Kellogg Saddle.

1.5 Pass over Westfall Knob.

2.7 Pass Novio Spring and waterfall.

3.4 The Butterfly Trail goes left; turn right onto the Crystal Spring Trail.

5.0 Pass Crystal Spring.

6.2 Arrive at the Crystal Spring Trailhead at the Old Mount Lemmon Road.

15 Aspen Trail

The Aspen Trail is a short but very scenic day hike to a viewpoint overlooking the rugged Wilderness of Rocks area and the Pusch Ridge Wilderness. This is another cool hike during summer, and a good place to see fall color as the aspens change in October.

Distance: 3.0-mile loop
Approximate hiking time: 2 hours
Difficulty: Easy
Trail surface: Dirt and rocks
Best season: Spring through fall
Water availability: None
Other trail users: Horses
Canine compatibility: Dogs allowed on leash

Fees and permits: None
Maps: USGS Mount Lemmon; USFS: Pusch Ridge Wilderness
Trail contacts: Coronado National Forest, Santa Catalina Ranger District, 5700 N. Sabino Canyon Rd., Tucson 85750; (520) 749-8700; www.fs.fed.us/r3/coronado/

Finding the trailhead: From the Sabino Canyon Visitor Center, turn left onto Sabino Canyon Road; drive south 4.4 miles, and then turn left onto Tanque Verde Road. Drive east 2.6 miles, and then turn left onto Catalina Highway. Stay on Catalina Highway (a fee is required, payable at the entrance station a few miles into the mountains) 37.9 miles, and then turn left onto Summerhaven Road. Drive 1.7 miles south through Summerhaven to the end of the road at the Marshall Gulch Trailhead. GPS: N32° 25.66688' / W110° 45.31245'

The Hike

From the trailhead, start the hike on the Marshall Gulch Trail, which ascends Marshall Gulch west past Huntsman Spring to Marshall Saddle and a multiple-trail junction.

Take the leftmost trail, the Aspen Trail, which heads south around Marshall Peak. There is an exceptionally good viewpoint on the small hill just southwest of the trail at 1.6 miles. From this vantage, you can see much of the well-named Wilderness of Rocks to the southwest. Continue the hike on the Aspen Trail, which heads east as it continues around Marshall Peak, then descends a ridge to return to the Marshall Gulch Trailhead.

Quaking aspen is the most widespread tree in North America. It grows at the highest elevations in the mountains of southern Arizona, favoring cooler, north-facing slopes as well as sheltered canyon bottoms. The tall, graceful trees are up to 1 foot in diameter and reach about 50 to 70 feet in height. The smooth, white bark makes a vivid contrast to the associated evergreen trees. The leaves, which are attached by thin, flexible stems, shimmer in the slightest breeze. During the fall, the deciduous leaves turn brilliant shades of yellow, orange, and red, often slashing entire mountainsides with color. Western aspens propagate via their root system, so the many hundreds of trees forming a stand are actually the same plant. They are often the first tree to grow back after a forest fire because young aspens can tolerate open sunlight better than most evergreen seedlings. Quaking aspen lives only about a hundred years, but the aspen groves provide shade for the longer-lived firs and spruces to get a start. By the time the aspens are reaching old age, the evergreen trees are already replacing them.

In many areas, aspen groves harbor arborglyphs, or historic tree carvings. Mostly done by sheepherders of Basque ancestry, many of the carvings date back fifty years or more. Subjects range from simple lists of names to detailed depictions of people, wildlife, and buildings. Aspen bark is soft

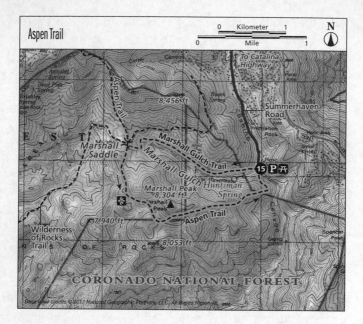

and easy to carve, but don't be tempted yourself. Old aspen carvings are historic artifacts protected by law, but there are far too many of us now to indulge in tree carving.

Miles and Directions

0.0 Leave the Marshall Gulch Trailhead on the Marshall Gulch Trail.

1.2 Reach Marshall Saddle and turn left onto the Aspen Trail.

1.6 Arrive at the viewpoint on the Aspen Trail.

3.0 Arrive back at the Marshall Gulch Trailhead.

16 Wilderness of Rocks

This long day hike leads from Mount Lemmon through the scenic Wilderness of Rocks and the Pusch Ridge Wilderness. Wilderness of Rocks takes its name from the many granite boulders, domes, cliffs, and other rock formations found in the area south of Mount Lemmon's summit.

Distance: 7.4-mile loop
Approximate hiking time: 5 hours
Difficulty: Moderate due to elevation change
Trail surface: Dirt and rocks
Best season: Spring through fall
Water availability: None
Other trail users: Horses
Canine compatibility: Dogs allowed on leash

Fees and permits: None
Maps: USGS Mount Lemmon; USFS: Pusch Ridge Wilderness
Trail contacts: Coronado National Forest, Santa Catalina Ranger District, 5700 N. Sabino Canyon Rd., Tucson 85750; (520) 749-8700; www.fs.fed.us/ r3/coronado/

Finding the trailhead: From the Sabino Canyon Visitor Center, turn left onto Sabino Canyon Road; drive south 4.4 miles, and then turn left onto Tanque Verde Road. Drive east 2.6 miles, and then turn left onto Catalina Highway. Stay on Catalina Highway (a fee is required, payable at the entrance station a few miles into the mountains) 40.4 miles to the end of the road at Mount Lemmon. GPS: N32° 26.42053' / W110° 47.20612'

The Hike

From the parking area, head west on the Mount Lemmon Trail, which skirts around the south side of the fenced Mount Lemmon Observatory and then heads southwest, descending on a broad ridge crest. You'll pass through Lemmon Park, which is a small meadow set in stands of ponder-osa pine, Douglas fir, limber pine, and white fir, and then pass the junction with the Quartzite Spring Trail, where a power line also meets the trail.

Hikers wanting an easy hike can turn left here and hike 0.3 mile to the Lemmon Rock Trail. From this junction, you could turn right and walk 0.2 mile to Lemmon Rock Look-out for the view and then backtrack to the junction and walk 0.3 mile to the Mount Lemmon Trailhead. The total distance of this loop is 1.7 miles.

To stay on the main loop, stay right on the Mount Lem-mon Trail and follow it southwest down the ridge and along the power line. Both the Sutherland Trail and the power line leave the ridge to the west; stay left on the Mount Lemmon Trail. For about 0.5 mile, the descent becomes steeper as the Mount Lemmon Trail drops down in a series of switchbacks, then levels out and works its way around several hills along the ridge. A final descent leads to a saddle and the Wilderness of Rocks Trail.

Turn left onto the Wilderness of Rocks Trail and follow it east and northeast into the headwaters of Lemmon Canyon. This area is known as the Wilderness of Rocks because of the large number of granite outcrops in the area. Mixed in with the ponderosa pine–Gambel oak forest, the rocks provide a delightful setting. Just east of the saddle, the trail descends to cross an unnamed tributary of Lemmon Canyon and climbs gradually over a broad ridge. A steeper, longer descent leads across another tributary. After this crossing, the Wilderness of Rocks Trail works its way across another broad ridge before dropping into upper Lemmon Canyon, which it follows to the junction with the Lemmon Rock Trail.

Turn left here and follow the Lemmon Rock Trail north. At first the trail climbs gradually, but soon the steep slopes of

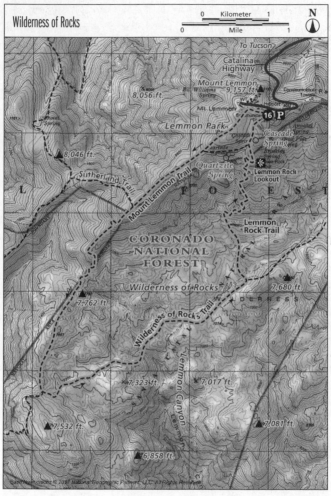

Mount Lemmon force the trail into a series of switchbacks. A huge rock outcrop to the west of the trail is called Rappel Rock because of the 200-foot overhang that allows climbers to do a long, free rappel. More switchbacks through the pine and oak forest lead to Lemmon Rock Lookout and one of the best views found anywhere in the Catalinas. A fire lookout building is staffed during times of high fire danger and commands a view of much of the Pusch Ridge Wilderness, including the Wilderness of Rocks that you've just traversed, as well as the Santa Catalina Front Range. In the distance you can see the Rincon, Santa Rita, Baboquivari, and Tucson Mountains, among many others.

Continue north on the Lemmon Rock Trail, passing the Quartzite Spring Trail, which comes in from the left, and follow the Lemmon Rock Trail up the final slopes to the Mount Lemmon Trailhead.

Miles and Directions

0.0 Leave the Mount Lemmon Trailhead on the Mount Lemmon Trail.

0.7 Pass the junction with the Quartzite Spring Trail; stay right on the Mount Lemmon Trail.

1.4 Pass the junction with the Sutherland Trail; stay left on the Mount Lemmon Trail.

3.2 Leave the Mount Lemmon Trail and turn left onto the Wilderness of Rocks Trail.

5.4 Leave the Wilderness of Rocks Trail and turn left onto the Lemmon Rock Trail.

6.9 Pass the Lemmon Rock Lookout.

7.1 Pass the Quartzite Spring Trail and remain on the Lemmon Rock Trail.

7.4 Arrive back at the Mount Lemmon Trailhead.

Rincon Mountains

Most of the Rincon Mountains lie in the Rincon District of Saguaro National Park, as do all the hikes in this section. This "Sky Island" range varies from 2,800 feet at the desert floor to 8,612 feet at Mica Mountain and encompasses four distinct life zones along the rise from desert scrub to fir forest. An extensive trail system covers the foothills and reaches to the summits. The Rincon Mountains form a sort of inverted L. A long ridge, Tanque Verde Ridge, rises from the Rincon Visitor Center area and ascends steadily east to culminate in the summit of Mica Mountain. From Mica Mountain, Heartbreak Ridge runs generally south, dipping to Happy Valley Saddle before rising to the range's second-highest peak, Rincon Peak.

Most of the trailhead directions for the hikes in this section start from the Rincon Visitor Center, a good place to visit for maps, books, and up-to-date trail information.

To reach the Rincon Visitor Center from central Tucson, head east on Broadway Road to Houghton Road and turn right. Drive south 2.7 miles, and then turn left onto Old Spanish Trail. Continue southeast 2.8 miles to the park and the Rincon Visitor Center turnoff, on the left.

From the north, exit I-10 at Valencia Road; turn left and drive 3.0 miles to Kolb Road. Turn left, go 1.7 miles, and then turn right onto Irvington Road. After 4.0 miles, turn left onto

Houghton Road; drive 1.0 mile, turn right onto Escalante Road, and drive 2.0 miles to Old Spanish Trail. Turn left; after 0.2 mile, turn right at the park and Rincon Visitor Center turnoff.

From the south, exit I-10 at Houghton Road and head north 7.9 miles to Escalante Road. Turn right and drive 2.0 miles to Old Spanish Trail. Turn left, drive 0.2 mile, and then turn right at the park and Rincon Visitor Center turnoff.

17 Garwood Trail

This is an easy and gorgeous walk through Sonoran Desert foothills to an old dam site. Before the Rincon Mountains were part of Saguaro National Park, ranchers occupied the area and improved many natural water sources in order to get water for their homes and their cattle.

Distance: 3.4 miles out and back
Approximate hiking time: 3 hours
Difficulty: Easy
Trail surface: Dirt and rocks
Best season: Fall through spring
Water availability: None
Other trail users: Horses
Canine compatibility: Dogs not allowed
Fees and permits: Entrance fee

Maps: USGS Tanque Verde Peak; National Geographic: Saguaro National Park
Trail contacts: Saguaro National Park, 3693 S. Old Spanish Trail, Tucson 85730; (520) 733-5158; www.nps.gov/sagu/index.htm
Special considerations: During the hot summer months, plan to hike early in the day and carry plenty of water.

Finding the trailhead: From Rincon Visitor Center, turn right onto Old Spanish Trail, which becomes North Freeman Road. Continue 3.6 miles, and then turn right onto East Speedway Boulevard. Continue 3.0 miles east to the end of the road at the Douglas Spring Trailhead. GPS: N32° 14.13021' / W110° 41.20393'

The Hike

From the Douglas Spring Trailhead, follow the Douglas Spring Trail east across the desert flats 0.3 mile, and then turn right onto the Garwood Trail. There are numerous side trails that cross and intersect, but stay on the Garwood Trail to its end, and then turn left onto the Carrillo Trail. Follow the Carrillo Trail up a hill and along the side of a small canyon to Garwood Dam. Look for pools of water in the canyon below the dam, which often persist through the dry season. An ability to spot small water pockets like these is one of the skills that experienced desert hikers, and especially backpackers, soon develop.

Garwood Dam is the goal for the hike, at a point offering views of the Rincon Mountain foothills as well as the desert

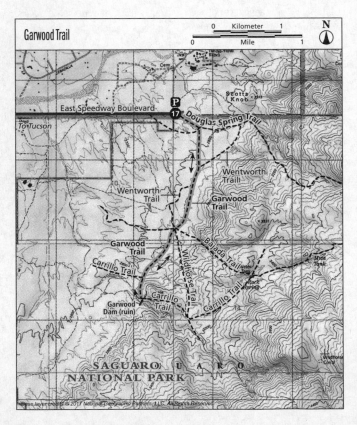

plain at their foot. The now-abandoned concrete dam was originally built across Wildhorse Canyon to supply water for a homestead. Notice how the saguaro cactus and scrub of the Lower Sonoran life zone give way to the grasslands of the Upper Sonoran life zone not too far above you. Other water improvements you may spot in the foothills of the Rincon Mountains include tanks and water troughs to catch and distribute water from springs, and windmills to pump water from wells.

Miles and Directions

0.0 Leave the Douglas Spring Trailhead and follow the Douglas Spring Trail east.

0.3 Leave the Douglas Spring Trail and turn right onto the Garwood Trail.

0.6 Pass the junction with the Wentworth Trail; stay right on the Garwood Trail.

0.7 Pass the second junction with the Wentworth Trail; stay left on the Garwood Trail.

1.1 The Bajada and Wildhorse Trails cross the Garwood Trail; remain on the Garwood Trail.

1.6 The Garwood Trail ends at Carrillo Trail; turn left onto the Carrillo Trail.

1.7 Arrive at Garwood Dam; return the way you came.

3.4 Arrive back at the Douglas Spring Trailhead.

18 Bridal Wreath Falls

Using the Douglas Spring Trail, this hike takes you to a seasonal waterfall in the foothills of the Rincon Mountains. The falls are most likely to be running during spring after a wet winter.

Distance: 5.2 miles out and back
Approximate hiking time: 4 hours
Difficulty: Easy
Trail surface: Dirt and rocks
Best season: Fall through spring
Water availability: None
Other trail users: Horses
Canine compatibility: Dogs not allowed
Fees and permits: Entrance fee

Maps: USGS Tanque Verde Peak; National Geographic: Saguaro National Park
Trail contacts: Saguaro National Park, 3693 S. Old Spanish Trail, Tucson 85730; (520) 733-5158; www.nps.gov/sagu/index.htm
Special considerations: During the hot summer months, plan to hike early in the day and carry plenty of water.

Finding the trailhead: From Rincon Visitor Center, turn right onto Old Spanish Trail, which becomes North Freeman Road. Continue 3.6 miles, and then turn right onto East Speedway Boulevard. Continue 3.0 miles east to the end of the road at the Douglas Spring Trailhead. GPS: N32° 14.13021' / W110° 41.20393'

The Hike

From the Douglas Spring Trailhead, hike east on the Douglas Spring Trail across the Sonoran Desert plain. Numerous trails branch right in this section; stay left on the Douglas Spring Trail at all of them. The easy section ends as the trail turns southeast and begins climbing a ridge in the foothills

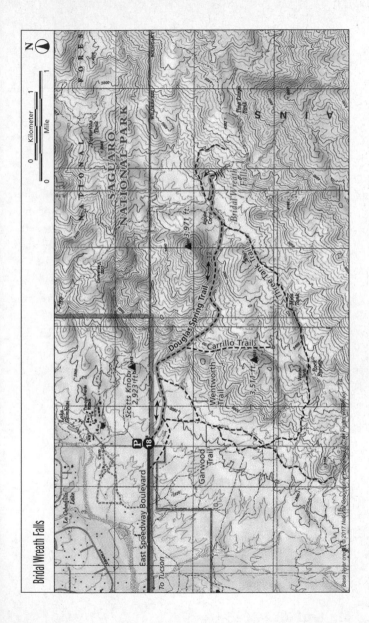

Bridal Wreath Falls

of the Rincon Mountains. Look back frequently for good views of the Tucson valley and, to the northwest, the Santa Catalina Mountains.

Eventually the trail drops into a ravine and turns back to the east. As the trail emerges onto a flat, you'll notice that the trail has climbed into the Upper Sonoran life zone. The saguaros are gone, replaced by the high-desert grassland characteristic of this life zone.

In 1989 lightning started a wildfire that eventually burned a large area on the north slopes of Tanque Verde Ridge, including the upper portion of the Douglas Spring Trail. Evidence of the fire is visible in the form of blackened brush and bits of charcoal, but it is remarkable how fast the landscape recovers from a wildfire.

Cottonwoods mark the drainage just south of the trail, where seasonal water sometimes surfaces. Just after passing the Three Tank Trail, turn right onto the Bridal Wreath Falls Trail, which goes south 0.4 mile into a small canyon. The falls are seasonal, and the best chances to see them running are after snowmelt in March and April, or after a thunderstorm during late summer.

Miles and Directions

0.0 Leave the Douglas Spring Trailhead and hike east on the Douglas Spring Trail.

0.3 Pass the Garwood Trail junction and remain on the Douglas Spring Trail.

0.5 Pass the junction with the Wentworth Trail and remain on the Douglas Spring Trail.

0.9 Pass the junction with the Carrillo Trail; stay left on the Douglas Spring Trail.

2.1 Pass the junction with the Three Tank Trail; stay left on the Douglas Spring Trail.

2.2 Turn right onto the unsigned Bridal Wreath Falls Trail.

2.6 Arrive at Bridal Wreath Falls; return the way you came.

5.2 Arrive back at the Douglas Spring Trailhead.

19 Cactus Forest Trail

This trail starts from the scenic loop drive and wanders north through gentle desert terrain past magnificent stands of saguaro cactus. The first portion of the trail, inside the scenic loop drive, is open to mountain bikers.

Distance: 8.4 miles out and back
Approximate hiking time: 5 hours
Difficulty: Moderate due to distance
Trail surface: Dirt and rocks
Best season: Fall through spring
Water availability: None
Other trail users: Horses, mountain bikes
Canine compatibility: Dogs not allowed
Fees and permits: Entrance fee

Maps: USGS Tanque Verde Peak; National Geographic: Saguaro National Park
Trail contacts: Saguaro National Park, 3693 S. Old Spanish Trail, Tucson 85730; (520) 733-5158; www.nps.gov/sagu/index.htm
Special considerations: During the hot summer months, plan to hike early in the day and carry plenty of water.

Finding the trailhead: From Rincon Visitor Center, turn right onto Cactus Forest Drive and go 0.9 mile to the Cactus Forest Trailhead (South) on the left. To reach the Cactus Forest Trailhead (North) (GPS: N32° 13.2474' / W110° 43.5565') from the Rincon Visitor Center, turn left onto Cactus Forest Drive and go 2.7 miles to the trailhead, on the left. To reach the Broadway Trailhead from the Rincon Visitor Center, turn right onto Old Spanish Trail, which becomes North Freeman Road. Continue 2.6 miles, and then turn right onto Broadway Boulevard. Drive 0.7 mile to the Broadway Trailhead, on the right. GPS: N32° 10.22090' / W110° 43.72600'

The Hike

Mountain bikers are allowed on the first portion of the trail, within Cactus Forest Drive. When you reach the Cactus Forest Trailhead (North), cyclists have the options of returning on the trail the way you came or turning right on one-way Cactus Forest Drive and following it back to the Cactus Forest Trailhead (South), a distance of 4.3 miles on the paved road.

From the Cactus Forest Trailhead (South), the Cactus Forest Trail wanders generally north through the gentle desert plain, winding through stands of tall saguaro cactus. If you left a shuttle vehicle at the Cactus Forest Trailhead (North), you'll have to complete the one-way loop drive by turning right.

The Cactus Forest Trail continues north across the road, and the Mesquite Trail soon comes in from the right. Stay left to the junction with the Mica View Trail, where you should stay right on the Cactus Forest Trail. At yet another junction, the Cholla Trail comes in from the right; stay left and follow the Cactus Forest Trail to the Shantz Trail, where you'll turn left and walk just 0.1 mile farther to the Broadway Trailhead. This is the end of the hike if you left a shuttle vehicle here; otherwise, return the way you came.

Look for several examples of dead and fallen saguaros, which reveal their inner structure. Unlike trees, saguaros are supported by a ring of woody, individual ribs just under the outer skin of the plant. The interior consists of a moist pulp, which is protected by the ribs. Unlike some desert plants, saguaros do not use deep groundwater to survive dry periods. Instead, these huge cacti have a shallow root system that collects water rapidly after rains. The entire plant expands as it stores water and gradually contracts as internal moisture is used.

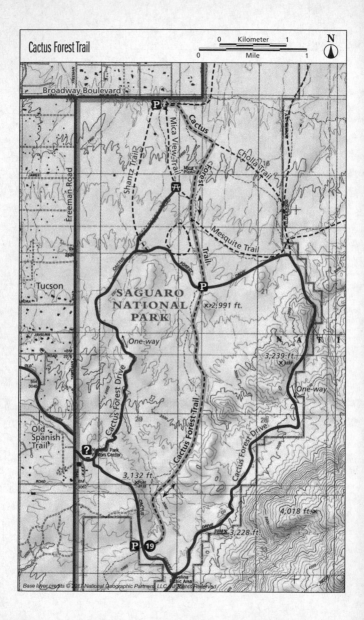

Because the shallow root system is incapable of supporting the plant, saguaros are literally balanced on their bases, which some people have found out the hard way after vandalizing a saguaro. In at least one highly publicized case, someone shot at a saguaro with a shotgun from close range. The cactus rocked back and forth a couple of times before falling on the perpetrator and killing him.

Heavy cattle grazing took place in the western foothills of the Rincon Mountains for many years, which had a severe impact on the saguaro cactus. Cattle destroyed the nurse trees on which young saguaros depend for survival, as well as trampling the saguaros themselves. As a result, the area of the Cactus Forest Trail is populated mostly with old saguaros.

Miles and Directions

0.0 Leave the Cactus Forest Trailhead (South) and hike north on the Cactus Forest Trail.

2.4 Pass the Cactus Forest Trailhead (North) and cross Cactus Forest Drive.

2.9 Pass the junction with the Mesquite Trail; stay left on the Cactus Forest Trail.

3.2 Pass the junction with the Mica View Trail; stay right on the Cactus Forest Trail.

3.4 Pass the junction with the Cholla Trail; stay left on the Cactus Forest Trail.

4.0 Cross the Shantz Trail; continue straight to remain on the Cactus Forest Trail.

4.2 Arrive at the Broadway Trailhead; return the way you came.

8.4 Arrive back at the Cactus Forest Trailhead (South).

20 Ridge View Trail

This is an easy walk to a viewpoint overlooking the rugged south slopes of Tanque Verde Ridge, the long west ridge of the Rincon Mountains that culminates in the 8,612-foot summit of Mica Mountain.

Distance: 1.8 miles out and back
Approximate hiking time: 2 hours
Difficulty: Easy
Trail surface: Dirt and rocks
Best season: Fall through spring
Water availability: None
Other trail users: Horses
Canine compatibility: Dogs not allowed
Fees and permits: Entrance fee

Maps: USGS Tanque Verde Peak; National Geographic: Saguaro National Park
Trail contacts: Saguaro National Park, 3693 S. Old Spanish Trail, Tucson 85730; (520) 733-5158; www.nps.gov/sagu/index.htm
Special considerations: During the hot summer months, plan to hike early in the day and carry plenty of water.

Finding the trailhead: From the Rincon Visitor Center, turn left onto Old Spanish Trail. Continue 7.2 miles, and then turn left onto Camino Loma Alta. Drive 2.4 miles north to the end of the road. GPS: N32° 08.00996' / W110° 41.24905'

The Hike

This easy hike in the Sonoran Desert foothills starts on the Hope Camp Trail, which is popular with horseback riders. After just 0.1 mile, you'll turn left onto the Ridge View Trail. The trail follows a dry wash with limited views for 0.8 mile, but then abruptly ends on a ridge with good views of the vast sweep of Tanque Verde Ridge as it climbs from the low desert to the northwest to the pine and fir forest of the Rincon high country around Mica Mountains and Rincon Peak.

Several varieties of cholla cactus grow in the foothills of the Rincon Mountains. One of the most common is teddy bear cholla, a fuzzy-looking yellow cactus with many branches that grows up to 6 feet tall. It looks cuddly, but it's best to keep your distance. The stems and joints are covered with hundreds of razor-sharp spines, each tipped with microscopic barbs. If an animal or human is unlucky enough to brush up against the cholla, the spines cling fiercely to skin or clothing. Since the ends of the stems break off easily, the resulting cholla balls are

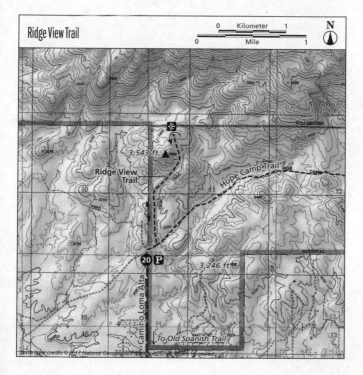

transported by animals to new locations, where, if conditions are favorable, a new plant will germinate.

Miles and Directions

0.0 Leave the Ridge View Trailhead and start on the Hope Camp Trail.

0.1 Leave the Hope Camp Trail and turn left onto the Ridge View Trail.

0.9 Arrive at the overlook at the end of the Ridge View Trail; return the way you came.

1.8 Arrive back at the Ridge View Trailhead.

Clubs and Trail Groups

Arizona Mountaineering Club
arizonamountaineeringclub.org

Arizona Trailblazers Hiking Club
www.azhikers.org

Arizona Trail Association
PO Box 36736
Phoenix, AZ 85067
(602) 252-4794
www.aztrail.org

Sierra Club, Grand Canyon Chapter
514 W. Roosevelt St.
Phoenix, AZ 85003
(602) 253-8633
www.sierraclub.org/arizona

Southern Arizona Hiking Club
www.sahcinfo.org

About the Author

The author has a serious problem: He doesn't know what he wants to do when he grows up. Meanwhile, he's done such things as wildland firefighting, running a mountain shop, flying airplanes, shooting photos, and writing books. He's a backcountry skier, climber, figure skater, mountain biker, amateur radio operator, river runner, and sea kayaker; but the thing that really floats his boat is hiking and backpacking. No matter what else he tries, the author always comes back to hiking—especially long, rough, cross-country trips in places like the Grand Canyon. Some people never learn. But what little he has learned, he's willing to share with you—via his books, of course, but also via his websites, blogs, and whatever else works.

His other FalconGuides include:

Basic Illustrated: Using GPS
Best Easy Day Hikes Albuquerque
Best Easy Day Hikes Flagstaff
Best Easy Day Hikes Las Vegas
Best Easy Day Hikes Sedona
Best Hikes Near Phoenix
Camping Arizona
Desert Hiking Tips
Explore! Joshua Tree National Park
Explore! Mount Shasta Country
Grand Canyon National Park Pocket Guide
FalconGuide to Saguaro National Park and the Santa Catalina Mountains
Hiking Arizona
Hiking Arizona's Superstition and Mazatzal Country

Hiking Northern Arizona
Hiking Oregon's Central Cascades
Joshua Tree National Park Pocket Guide
Mountain Biking St. George and Cedar City
Mountain Biking Phoenix

American Hiking Society is the only national voice for hikers—dedicated to promoting and protecting America's hiking trails, their surrounding natural areas, and the hiking experience.

At American Hiking Society, we work hard so you can play! We advocate for families who love to hike, and we support communities who are creating new opportunities for your trail family to get outside. Hiking is a great way to bond with your kids, parents, grandparents, neighbors, or even furry friends.

Come with us on the trail and listen to the sweet sound of bird songs and look high into the boughs of old oak trees. We'll help you develop an active lifestyle, learn about the wonders of nature, and become a steward of your favorite trails. So grab your hiking shoes, a well-stocked daypack, partner, kids, friends, parents, and dogs— and get outdoors!

Become a member of the national hiking community
at www.americanhiking.org. Join today!